What Is Owed?

Kelwyn Sole

Some of these poems have been published previously in: Botsotso, New Coin, Johannesburg Review of Books, Global Voices Now.

Acknowledgments:
Adonis *selected poems* (New Haven: Margellos/Yale University Press, 2010); Amiri Baraka *Selected Poetry of Amiri Baraka/LeRoi Jones* (New York: William Morrow, 1979); Jim Harrison *Complete Poems* (Port Townsend: Copper Canyon, 2021); Federico García Lorca *Collected Poems* (New York: Farrar, Straus and Giroux, 2001); Nigel Penn *Rogues, Rebels and Runaways* (Cape Town: David Philip, 1999); Wole Soyinka (ed.) *Poems of Black Africa* (London: Heinemann, 1975).

Grateful thanks for help to:
Allan Kolski Horwitz, Rochelle Kapp,
Karen Press, Stephen Symons and John Trimbur.

First published in 2025 by Botsotso

59 Natal St
Bellevue East 2198
Johannesburg

ISBNS
Print: 978-0-6398785-2-2
E-pub: 978-0-6398785-4-6

Design and typesetting: Stephen Symons
Set in Sabon 10/15pt

In the text © Kelwyn Sole

For Rochelle

You will linger on pathways
Where your forefather ran blindly
  - Jean Baptiste Tati-Loutard

The cost of flight is landing.
  - Jim Harrison

O childish poet, smash your clock!
  - Federico García Lorca

CONTENTS

The house	10
Those teenage years	14
It's the small things	16
The leader's speeches	18
We, briefly	20
How we live	20
How we think	23
Mall	25
Identity politics	26
Drosters	27
Spirit voices	29
Now silent (Gaza)	30
Early morning rain	34
Dawn	35
If you wake up	36
Zen in the art of birdwatching	38
Letter to the editor	42
The Spyder	46
Farmlands	48
What lurks there	49
After	54
Sharon	56
Sushi syntax	58
Groot Constantia	60
Mooning the moon *(to be taken as read)*	64
Song	65
Shadowed	66

Touching dawn	67
Two American adventures	70
Massachusetts in review	70
Brand	72
Laureates, at sea	73
The reader's hypocrite	75
Monk, dancing	77
Poetry	79
Poems of need	79
Weed	82
Beasts	83
Word perfect	85
Clunkerfoot	88
Night ward	89
What ocean	90
Mirror lost	91
With no moment's thought	93
Stepping out	94
Leaving comfort	94
Against dead reckoning	95
Oasis	96
As you pass by	97
What is (ode)	98
Gaze	106
Author Biography	107

*A gate opens: I do
not know whether
my task is to close it,
or go through.*

The house

1

A child remembers a house
close to the beach
                high on its own dune
strangled by concrete and tar, looking out
over shipwrecks and whales and the many
seasons of nude human flesh:
                        held by a maze
of walls and rooms and corners, he found he
could never sidestep the doting eyes of adults
to dance his own dance, betrayed to them
each time by the dribbles of sand he forgot
to wash off his feet

            so there was a world
       he rarely saw,
tricked by the ego of childhood, willing to ignore
the angles as they shifted around him, their shadows
failing daily to run away from a relentless sun
until even he felt secure,
                    when enclosed.

There were others who'd been there before:
an old chair in one corner seemed to rock itself
to sleep, and the gleam of plastered walls
bore the sigils of so many cockroaches and beetles
that had been crushed by a hand, some hand
no one would admit to

      though with their rituals
of wine, and the solace of coffee nightly on
their tongues, the adults encircled each other
and gossiped to rebut the cold, dark distances in
which the galaxies he saw offered up their light.

2

Outside, thick entanglements of bitou
and milkwood provoked his fear to flare
and flourish – with cries cut short, a stifled
rustle, nothing he could see:
        or sinuous
green lengths of garden hose might insinuate
themselves, only to slither imperceptibly
away …

     was that you, head downward
on the beach, bent over a shrapnel of shells:
dogwhelks, tritons, screw shells and – once –
the perfect forsaken architecture of a paper
nautilus
     while behind, in its endless roar,
salt questioned your life through the rhythms
of the sea
     and crumbled, grain by grain,
the fragile certainties of your land?

3

This time there's red tide in the bay:
ugly smears of rust spread across the water,
sand littered with gasping fish and dead crabs.
The night is bewitched:
                        in the dark
waves glow and flicker a blue florescence
that surfs and sparks in sight for hours.

He stays awake, the man returned, to see. Though
hearing is another thing: that rumble that somehow
still can't stir   a house asleep –

until at length morning brings its dough of clouds
fluffing up into a bread of promise above
long-crusted soil;
                      the sweet peas fastened
to the wall as always tumble their colours
down the stone.

                  Perhaps, he thinks,
what he wants to hold fast here are just
fractals of happiness that ghost around
then sheer away,
                    their colours long bleached
by the unremitting verticals and perpendiculars
of a life endured
                    by him and others his by blood
far beyond a rickety family table

4

The house now empty watches all:
things move towards what has become
a mollusc- and gannet-diminished sea
that reaches out to nowhere.

Nowhere to come to rest
                in a country
no one is allowed to name
except in beauteous language

even if
        in its forgotten passages
                        the bare
soles of his childhood still chafe incessantly.

Those teenage years

I'm in trouble here
and it's all your fault, you

with your ordinary, preoccupied face

who strolls past me and everyone
and
your air of panache
and
dirty, tied-back hair
and
flecks of henna and dandruff
                                      so that I

stumble
        behind my hands

lower them, lift them, lower
them to my sides again
can't remember what they're for

– one pierced eyebrow flirting
with light,
            your legs
protrude their knees
too bonily for the routines
of beauty
            lips not quite sure
of the coolest way

to cant that
cigarette –

but I don't care

(should I say hi?)

for suddenly all the words of those songs
on the radio I've tried to memorise
look up at me anew with your freckles
and mismatched eyes, frogs
from the bottom of a pond,
    when you pass:

    but your heels wave
their cracked pink backs at me, one
by one, to say goodbye

receding to a place
I can no longer see them

   and that's because

you climb on your scooter, glance at me
once,
  frown,
    pout,
      then putter off.

It's the small things

Lost to my focus is the dazzle of colours of roses and carnations, and the yellow eyes of the Barberton Daisies, fluttering their white lashes despite the blister beetles tormenting them

nor can I build any meaning out of lawns that rise, tier after tier, from low front hedge to high back wall, the latter studded with broken glass.

Nothing coheres, from my perspective. I am only three foot tall.

I'd like to hear better, discover more: but all that comes is a single gush of air expelled from someone's lungs, and a distant imprecation –

soon I will see a snake head, separated from its body; and a spade leaning against a fence. My father says it's a Night Adder, and venomous: biting out of whim.

I will work out later that the broken shape in front of me ate only eggs, and is our neighbour's lost lamented pet.

These small things come to define my parents' garden.

The leader's speeches

1

The leader's speeches slide into our ears
like grease,
        and clog,
                so we scratch ourselves
again, again, with the tickle of his promises;
till we are soothed in our knowledge
that they're evasions, that nothing changes.

I'm reminded of the lungfish, beslimed
and blundering, which at each drought's onset
digs into the drying mud to wait – hoping to
become invisible – for the rains it prays may,
just may, come.
        Just so
                he starts to estivate,
po-faced. Then he remembers: and a smile
wickers across his features its brief electricity.
Yet only his followers can be lit up for long
with this iteration, the routine pledges none
but they suppose will ever be fulfilled.

Our cities crumble, and those given them
in guardianship bicker in their greed
                          as the old
slogans of liberation peel their paint and crack,
shopworn and potholed as the ruins of commerce

and supply our country has become. We moulder
in disbelief at what keeps happening; though
each one keeps tweeting urgent and compulsive
supplications to the online gods, to take note
of our individual, ersatz, temporary survival.

For what else can we do? No one seems
to know, or be able to imagine, the future;
so continues to spell out our private void
in the middle of calamity
                              into infinity.

2

There's blight and mildew
                    of neglect
on our memories of past heroes now frozen
into statues because the lichen of the leader
and his Party clings corrosively to everything.

On every screen the pixels reviving the faces
that lived history are buffered to mythologies:
their courage endured through
blood and pain, misspoken.

                        All around us
we see freedom's cuckoos grown and fattened
in nests of tenders and deployments

and the birdshit beggars belief.

We, briefly

How we live

After waking,
the homeless shuffle down the street
having slept fitfully in our legacy:
a bed of pitilessness.

* * *

A scorpion of wind, lashing its tail
through drowsing houses, basks
surreptitiously in sun.

* * *

Then it rains, and there is

clear water off the mountain
instant waterfalls alongside the road
a stream that wavers, then reasserts itself

debouched into drains and sewers.

* * *

She folded her spirit inside her
like it was a letter, until it was
enveloped in her skin
Is this mine?
        and sealed it with
her spittle of disappointment.

– So it was done to every daughter,
just as you might guess.

* * *

Beetling up the hill

rows of plush apartment blocks

– mostly empty, mostly owned

by rich and transient foreigners –

rattle their air conditioners

in endless gossip.

* * *

Some rise at noon. The land bends
its back down under a burden of hope,
expectations bound in skin,
gristle, the sinews of
our facsimiles of
              desire.

     Our earth
is a tired, sweating muscle
that labours in vain as it tries
to help maintain the malign
work of monied hands.

* * *

Why must dogs with different owners
incessantly praise each other,
despite the fences in between?

* * *

Afternoon is kicked down the street
in a final *tjank* of light.
The white takkies of a man scurrying
along pushing an empty pram
that he tries to fill from
dustbin after dustbin
      gleam
between each newborn shadow,
cast by a regiment of streetlights
 into brief whimpers of radiance.

* * *

Cloned shopfronts
glitter in the setting sun

– the question
      now, the question is,
how much longer are we going to buy it?

* * *

Nightfall.

A hired hitman gifts
a passing child

in error

with a third eye
in the middle
of her forehead.

How we think

With battlements of swift opinions
we hoard our illusions,
spoonfeeding our own mouths
              yet stay
autocorrected all our lives.

* * *

The bright recognition of the self
through words everyone creates for themselves
with a cellphone held up to their features
incurs nothing. The face is not a book.

* * *

The earth is closing in on us
who are closed in. But we'll
deny it
      with concrete words
and the footpaths that profit
from leading nowhere,
          from
bestowing nothing as their goal.

* * *

These days
      our souls
end up
as concrete
      forgetting the sand,
      forgetting the water,
      of their making.

Mall

Yelled at by
his white boss

for making
an americana

instead of
a flat white

his grip is
unsteady as

he hands me
(next in line)

a trembling
styrofoam cup.

Identity politics

I'll tell you exactly
what I think

just so long

as my words
don't offend you.

Drosters

> *Fugitives (drosters) were ... the true pioneers of the colonial frontier. They were always in search of the outer limits of the colony in order to pass beyond them. In so doing, paradoxically, they served only to extend the colonial frontier, for they, unwittingly, took the colony with them.*

I fled the Dutch East India Company, but was captured.

I fled the slave bell, but was captured.

I fled that long distance to the mountains of Die Galg, but was betrayed and captured.

I fled the whip was hunted down by pain and captured.

I fled to Madagascar but took the wrong path found the wastelands and was captured.

I fled the magistrates, but was captured.

I killed the farmer who had my woman, but was burnt with her after we were captured.

I had the flesh pinched out from my body with red hot tongs a noose already round my neck because I was and always will be captured.

I fled what the meester called *this earthly coil*, but the memory of me was captured.

I fled the *rooineks*, but was captured.

I fled the slumyards, but was captured.

I fled Verwoerd, but was captured.

I fled Sun City, but was captured.

I fled the Party, but was captured.

I fled those who smiled at me from their enormous mansions, but by them was soothed and captured.

I fled the compradors grunting and wheedling for scraps at their troughs; but along with them, I'm captured.

I fled the copyright laws, but was captured

I fled the glitter of brand names, but was captured and branded on that wheel.

I fled the words of all who want to name me, but was worn out on my journey by the endless route markers along this page

and so I am still captured. When will I find

the trail that leads me out so

I no longer can be captured?

Spirit voices

There seem to be no forefathers left
except for those stuck in our minds –

then I think: their bones festering
under our infertile, powdery soil

still shout out to us, a reminder of
their hopes
                left unfulfilled.

Now silent (Gaza)

Swiftly darting silver needle
warplane

scratches itself
                across
the cornea of the blue sky,

and mine. Until, half-blinded,
I cannot foretell

the trajectory of its bombs –
where they will burst,

or whose will be the flesh
smashed into gobbets.

I want to catch these missiles
on my tongue, and try to

defuse them with my words,
knowing it is futile.

*   *   *

A man, with mouth silently agape,
gathers up his baby rendered
almost unrecognisable,
skin crisped into crackling:

one more tiny body
flopped down in what once
was a street, one
of so many
           with heads and legs
           crushed in, or missing.

* * *

Cities where mothers cannot stop keening,
and children do not break their hearts from
crying, but shatter into many pieces more.

We search for their limbs in rubble.

Early morning rain

After the climb
suddenly

a pool
      pulsing like a heart
on the rock body of the mountain

where tadpoles vie
to nibble away
          the shimmering
meniscus of dawn.

Dawn

He watched it dying. Deepbodied, a Socratic thinker's brow, like nothing else he's seen. Reddish, but with a blue spot a smudge under the eye and a sheen – was it golden? - around the gills. He had expected the colours to fade after death but that's not what happened. Its skin seemed to flutter, then strobe through wave after wave of colour: green, pink, blue, even as it gasped, and its eyes stilled in surrender.
- *What's that fish?*
- *It's a dageraad. Don't tell anyone I caught this, please, it's not allowed.*
- *Never heard of it. That's Afrikaans?*
- *Neh. It's Dutch, I think ... 'dawn'. You just saw why.*
That night, nothing else to do, he googled until he found the ichthyologist Margaret Smith, on youtube or vimeo or whatever, who remarked that '*Chrysoblephus cristiceps* is the most beautiful of all creatures, as waves of different colours pass over the body in death'. So, a fish of revivifying beauty even in extreme agony? Increasingly, as he read, he imagined it some sort of visitor, a sign, a blessing he could not quite decipher: because, long-living as it was, after a certain size the individuals changed from female to male. All this seemed miraculous to him, a miracle fish; this, once so abundant on reefs around the coast. Equally mind-numbing the fact that, within a decade and half, ninety-five percent of the species in South African waters had been fished out.
He looked past the busy, bent, intent figure, out to where the horizon turned into an uncertainty of haze. Not at sea. At sea. We are all at sea now, choking, where the dawn's promise is erasing its colours on the scales of the sky.

If you wake up

If you wake up to sound, then your day
will be lucky. Your bed may be empty
but first light will be faithful:
                              if you're quiet,
you will hear all that is not human heave up
from distant mountains on wings, whispering
a beginning that transitions from red, to yellow;
the whirr and flight of the sun insect-like
into the morning.
                    Coeval nations of a planet,
creatures to the quick, we must all follow
in our body carapaces of skin or fur or shell
and (we all know this summoning to life!)
breathe in, then out: the embouchure of dawn.

Bedazzled, it's time to forget the longing
for tales of horizons of sea and sky, but focus
more closely:
                    bees are singing morning into light
though the flowers want to doze and nod their heads
for just a few more seconds. Bees sing the morning
into their steady business, bumbling with purpose,
butting aside the protestations of any calyx
coquettish enough to jar open with a promise of
undiscovered treasure beneath. Each petal flaunts
a different colour, with the sum of it a unity
that yells out summer, summer!

                              The bees sing
and by their song now my tongue finds itself surprised
as if coated with pollen, lured to a beauty that tricks
words into becoming suitors or blushing brides.

Pollen dusts the tongue. Though I can't insert mine
into the bell of this lily to know what it's like,
the chamber hiding that special taunt of sweetness
flowers harbour. The incongruity of my stooping,
a heartsick old primate prayerful and exact
in front of every colour he can seek to find
and many that he can't. Here I am, my mask
of refusal slipping, pollen dusting all my face.

There are rumours bees will pass from our world.
Perhaps; but the only merciful part of this for me
is to be selfish. It's enough for once if today I
can stand attuned to their tiny miracle, hearing
the hum of living go on and on,
                                        at least for now.

Bees have saved and nourished us always –
what a dire time this is, that humans must talk
of saving bees!
                    Benighted, death-bearing drone,
I won't get up from kneeling down among them
despite my cracking joints and arthritis
as I celebrate and mourn all at once
the dying of a world I cannot help but love.

Zen in the art of birdwatching

There is no ignorance, and no end to ignorance.
- Heart Sutra

1

To start: lose that GPS (for good)
and throw away that bird list: the bird
finds you, not you the bird: and then

wave away that anxiety, your compulsion
in your quest for birds – why is it there,
to give your life some hidden purpose?

Now you've identified another one: a lifer;
aren't you lucky? All that I can say is, well,
good for you: tell all your friends on twitter!

But are you good at species' names? At what
the primaries can tell you, or the cere?
Have you pored, jaw open, over pictures,

striving to set your mind at rest as to what
distinguishes a Shikra from a Goshawk
or from a Hobby; the jizz of A opposed to B?

I hate to say: this way, you've learned too little;
the less the more you learn. For beyond art,
beyond knowing, birds are those beings that flee,

taunt your attempts at seeing them. So there's
no better time than now to lower that phallic lens
(besides, your perfect shot flew out of frame!)

and use your eyes instead.

2

For somewhere, today,
a Burkea flushes its Hyliotas out into the wind;
a Trogon turns its back and vanishes into a forest;

or lurching, all at sea, you're in a world teeming
with Gannets that twist in the air to plunge down
around you, stockbrokers avid for panicked silver

(you didn't notice? did vomit incommode you?).
Elsewhere, a Kestrel hovers at noon, wingtips
smouldering alight till they pulse pure flame;

or against a setting sun, a Thrush in silhouette
hectors the last skin from an apple, and is gone
… if you wish, fill in the gaps here with what you

yet crave to find. Bird after bird after bird,
reduced to a tick by its name on a pencilled list
your grandchildren will glance at, then recycle.

3

I see you tweeting: *'the bird performed well!'*
but far as I can tell, *you* didn't. While you stared,
what magnitudes of space round it did you sense,

what field of view? Some birds, their eyes out-
smarting ours, see much more widely all around
than we ever could. So how can the edges

of your sight detect what may come, then go?
As the SUVs flock past, migrating to the place
they hope next to scry and possess what's rare

duck down, so none of them can see you.
Why chase after them?

4

                    Instead, welcome what
is common, perched timidly right in front of you.

There sits, for a second but in memory a lifetime
all that you know, and all you need to know.
In that instant, be quiet, and watch. Be branch. Be tree.

If it settles nearer, quieten your breath, but leave it
be to leave you. Greet the chance that gives grace
to you to meet   a life that's just itself.

*… As if the world around you were for this one day
infinite, precisely where you stand, with the clarity
of a summer tossing doves and hawks and feathers*

*up into the air; raptor indistinguishable from prey,
with your eyes and ears aligned with what are
the mere split-seconds from dawn to sunset … .*

If you want to stretch your palms towards a bird,
do so unencumbered. Carry nothing but who you
are. Ready to find surprise, then be filled anew

with wonder. This is the learning that birds bring:
brief moments which, like them, veer and scatter.
So be still, and wait. For whatever may come next.

Letter to the editor

Dear sir: *it's taken me a long while
to summon the courage to say this*,
but I would like to complain about
our local baboons
                      especially those
that have taken to loitering around
Adamastor Bakery. *Should this be
allowed to go on?* For one: my wife
no longer feels safe when she sends
our maid out to buy a loaf of bread

… and, to explain a little further …
our lovely, quiet, clever daughter
(who is the apple of both our eyes)
has of late taken to applying red
nail polish – overly garish, you
should see it! - to her, um, rear
and now makes revolting sounds,
smacking her lips each time
any male trundles into view …

we're also worried about our son
who's hooked up with a, um,
homely girl, despite the years
we slaved away to send him
to yet another good school
each time he was expelled …

our fear is that the two of them
may feel a need to knuckle down
to, to, who knows what improper
lifestyle? Or even, heaven help us,
begin a family? For example:
I found them late last night,
trying out ways to mate on top
of the Land Cruiser I've bought...

and what's more, the ill-permed
little hussy won't stop dropping
hints that she'd like to become
bride to his groom - says she's
tickled pink the way he grooms:
while, as for him, he tells us that
he thinks they'll be hirsuted
(*I tell him, sorry my boy, I
really don't find that funny...*).

What's more, it would take me
hours to talk about her endless
relatives, who're now so eager
to ape our every move, shop
at the places where we shop,
scratching out good bargains
as they go
        not excluding what
they might find upon each other

and, furthermore, I can't begin
to tell you how annoying those
family picnics have become, as
her granny will see fit to raise
those bushy eyebrows in what
appears to be (*can you believe
it!*) a semblance of aversion –
it's clear she judges us, yes,
us, no equal to her family –
(*we're not* de troop *enough,
it seems; unable, in her view
to root out a decent living*).

I'm concerned that they may
soon start to invade the garden,
my games room, our jacuzzi,
claiming to be some sort of
'*rightful owners*' of my land,
just because that troublemaking
old biddy from down the road
once told them that they were
indigenous. I ask you! If I use
my cricket bat to drive them out,
will they throw rocks, find ways
to traumatise our dog and cat,
rip out the shrubs that we've so
carefully nurtured, for years?
– *And no, I don't care if they
tell me that they're tasty!*

And then? What then? Where's
our Neighbourhood Watch now
that we need them? I know
I won't be able to stop them,
or phone the City Council

as even the Red Ants seem
already to have been eaten ... .

The Spyder

Apologies to William Blake

Spyder, Spyder, crawling light
On the bedspreads of the night:
What mere mortal skin or eye
Can'st bear to know Thee skulking by?

In what domestic cavity
Do'st please thee now to squeeze and pry?
Foul villain, octopedal blight,
In what chink hide'st Thee from mortal sight?

What roll'd newspapers, what poison arts,
Can'st sunder Thee to constituent parts?
On what tarsal claws creep'st Thou now nigh?
Can'st Thou tell Brackenfell Nymph from fly?

In crack-house squats 'neath Sea Point lamps,
In Noordhoek's oozy littoral swamps,
At fleamarkets, she lives in fear,
Doubts not Thy hairy soul draws near …

In Fish Hoek? – ah, the truth will out –
Manifesting from a shower's spout
Thy presence looms – a shriek! Dismayed,
Her ablutions flees the uncloth'd maid!

Drear Lord of Dark Satanic Mills,
She dreads Thy clacking mandibles:
Attend her still! Be one of her pets!
What palps! What fangs! What spinnerets!

When dismal night unfolds to day
Perforce all vampires slink away
But thee - did'st He who, without ado,
Make Teletubby make Thee too?

Spyder, spyder, grizzly fright
'Cross sleeping *'s soles at night;
What mere mortal skin or eye
Durst not flinch, Thee skittering by?

Insert your name here

Farmlands

One dead tree,
and the stubble
still left after
harvest

      where
a sedge of cranes
opens the creaking door
of their voices.

What lurks there

When the beast screams next to your heart,
there is no auction of appeasement: no fruit
to be plucked, no serpent to blame, and you
will never dwell in a version of Eden.

The wolf in my dreams is tamed on
waking:
        no scent comes any longer
to intrigue it, and its tongue lollops,
protrudes,
        covers those canines

… for brief minutes it may
even appear to smile …

until the villagers, oblivious of danger,
do not realise where it is as they pass;
forget to watch the shadows in which
it may seem to be asleep.

Shammer, he-who-hides-through-his-tongue,
a praise singer might declaim,
if a wolf were ever likely to find
anyone stupid enough to praise it –
what a quick tongue it has:
what a smirk it hides! …

* * * *

The gloom retreats from leaf to leaf,
scrambles backwards out of each bush,
flows away, and the grasses brighten
though not with day

because any wolf brings
the foreknowledge of those beasts
who see in the dark:
the grey, hidden sadness
of the world as it is.

This is the dole of the wolf.

* * * *

At times, for brief moments,
caution may not ambush it,
and an eerie eclát shines through
as it pants on fresh trails; makes
its own shadow a loyal watchdog
behind it
        even if every being
that lives in the forest, even
its victims, still murmur
in the gloom it casts
outside its path

though wary of it   still they know

that – in this civilising world – anything
that's been named as wolf
eventually gets its comeuppance.

* * * *

Yet there is something fragile
in the fierce purpose of a wolf:
how, as night presses down,
it's forced to howl out
the nightmare of darkness
newly gathering

lays itself
bare to proclaim

how cold the wind is
once the tracks have been lost;
how a splinter of moonlight
goads the belly onwards,
though seldom enough
to capture
quarry:

      that time when a wolf
must follow its nose.

*   *   *   *

But for now   just this spoor   entering darkness.

After

Sappho and Propertius

The ghost of none but her
came to me in a dream:
a ghost

      to me only,
these last ten years,

though she's not yet gone,
not earthmired

– *so what is lost?*

This –

a slight blush
blazing forth
on her cheeks
each time she smiles

the lock of hair
that flops
its black comma
into
      her eyes
as she laughs

a mole
 on her breast
moving
 slightly
if she gasps ...

sweet mouth smell

two moist tongues
feigning
combat

 : all else
I have forgotten.

Sharon

The foghorn's slow bombastic bleat just
before dawn. But she's close to blinded
every time the lighthouse glares at her,
leers into the room through the window
not quite closed in one corner.
                              Sprawled
small body blotted out by a mêlée of sheets,
the syncopations of nightlife in their clamour
and colours leave merely a judder, a flicker
to scratch blobbed pastilles beneath her lids.
The bed groans again each time she stirs

– he's gone. She slept through his going,
man no longer young, with placating words
which never turn out to be the right ones.
The freckles round her collarbone stand out
like letters branded onto a pale parchment
of skin
        at each sudden flourishing of light.
She can guess how his knuckles will tighten
on the wheel as he peers drunkenly through
the windshield – that belated swerve around
a limping dog! – and wonders if he'll find
any new excuse for the drowsy wife whom,
he says, no longer listens, nor even cares.

Can she ever get her soul to sign a statement
with her body, to stand up and say no, to
anything?
      When the sun rises (who knows?)
she may find an urge to falter to a doorway;
choose steps to lead her out to love that vast
diffused stain of sky that blends with sea
and its many ceaseless shapes that flinch
past overhead, whitely silent on their wings.
It may be too late to escape these whooping
ghosts of revelry into hope, or even oblivion –
and today may not offer up a single shadow
deep enough to hide all of her wishes inside –

but maybe there's another Sharon, not yet born,
inside the seamless blue eggshell of the world.

Sushi syntax

    sashimi sit redly on their board
        like freshly stopped hearts

       slopped soy on the table
         a shallow lake spreads
browns your sleeve
            engulfs gingham squares of green-on-white
one by one

the air steams between us
two spoons leaning
almost erect

(we're already
in our cups)

there's a glare behind your head
            the dazzling blue page of the sea
    a pier running into it
        like an exclamation mark

two far spy-hopping whales
counterfeit a brief quotation

           dipping gulls
    eye your plate
cackle bombast try to
submerge your words

> *one cappuccino*
> *one black coffee*
> *and the bill …*

         you grimace
       reach out
     until

holding hands we
stroll next to

this tourist menu called '*Sea*'
      making its grammar
           an escape route.

Groot Constantia

1

On the vineyards' edge we sit

where purple and yellow flowers
do not clash, you say, despite
their being on opposite sides
of the colour wheel. So
all things are and will be
– even as they collide –
disposed. Restaurant muzak,
waiters who orbit tourists:
vines stripped of their grapes,
and fishponds where reeds
begin to wilt

                but there are
unquiet ghosts at large here:
an insistent sibilance of voices
not dulled by time,
                     their pain
the scaffolding on which
the foundations of this city
founder still
            even if
only a single slave bell
now remains, muted,
dangling by its throat
from a newly painted arch.

2

The mountain looms,
an ampitheatre: rears up
aeons of stone
         that close in,
seem to watch the day's remains
slink its shadows past around us.

A jungle of pruned pleasure
on land stolen centuries before –
whitewashed walls that want
to build themselves ever higher –

in this dotage of summer
the city continues to blare
its whiteness
         in sonorities of coin,
a haggling of cars,

the clink of tourist-throttled wine
as the waiters come and go,
summoned to be polite to money.

3

We are two creatures surrounded
by our own flesh, squatting here
with a breeze delving sly fingers
in between

   our lives of havoc
and memories of havoc dissected
and displayed, stretched out
at a tangent
to good sense and reality ...

and we both have a real need to flee

4

desire. It eats you from the core
outwards. There is no recompense
for this.

   Craving lodges pips
in back of my throat,
a compulsion to chew, then
swallow.

   I am now your apple?

5

I don't know where we
go from here. All I know
is that I must

keep my poise, make idle
chatter and be lulled; be
quiet enough

              to watch the evening
start to spill its paint across
this fastidious Cape landscape
to render it
              transformed, and
turning black.

Mooning the moon

(to be taken as read)

In this summer as fires threaten
it has to be declared: my house
has become the colour of
sunsets.

Red walls. Red bedstead. A mirror
that will dissolve your features
– please come in! – to a subtle pink
contagion.

There's even a friend, Alizarin:
who visits at least once a week
for rooibos and redder than red
wine.

Each day my garden blossoms:
disas, a weeping boer-bean, some
bergamot. A sky blatant with its
sunrose

that sunburns. At night, were I to
flash my buttocks out the window,
they'd surely glow, twin neon
bulbs.

Song

Softness, softness
breast alighting on my palm
each bird hidden in the forest
begins at last to sing

Blindness, blindness
I cannot see your face
so speak to me those words
you will not give to others

Stillness, stillness
breaths slowing in the dark
under these cold stars
desire still builds its fire

Sweetness, sweetness
my body feeds with yours
within one tiny room
swelling to fill all space

Deftness, deftness
the labour of our fingers
disentangles every clock
till all of time is opened

Shadowed

for R.

Today I'm taking grief on my back
and trudging with it, finding my way
to the top of your mountain with its gift
of constant sunlight
                      as if it were no weight,
                            at all.

Touching dawn

1

The sea, a beehive of light:
wavecrests briefly scintillate,
shake themselves free in search
of the honey of the sun,
itself a blossom risen –

                a sound
that grumbles then is stilled
                      winds

turn, seek new directions: backwash
scrabbles each time to lose the shore
which clings, regardless, to
each whitened fingertip.

Also, here: this other daybreak
where I, who can hardly see
                  past
steam rising from my teacup
                      find
you still, right next to me.

2

I am turned around by you,
by these immensities: buoyant
in all weathers, the love
we've learned to trust
within us and about us

                        even more than
fulfilled desire
            comes
                    a fresh surprise:
the tides of joy we find
when our fingers
merely touch.

Two American adventures

Massachusetts in review

Emily Dickinson lived most of her days
within one room. But that's okay;
when she finally got to leave,
she got to leave for good.

– Do you know you can sing her poems
to the tune of 'Yellow Rose of Texas'?
There's even a website dedicated
to finding more to fit her metres ....
(my favourite? – 'House of the Rising Sun').

I croon this on my rented bike
(*Beecoz ... I could ... not stop ... for death*)
between picking up milk and laundry
(*He glaaa ... dly stopped ... for me!*)
as I wobble past Amherst's huge frat houses –
alpha sigma blah blah all mod cons.

Just down the road
a thin sculpture of beaten iron
shows her tête-à-tête with Robert Frost.
I'm told it's art, and that it doesn't matter
that they never met.
                       Mind you,

if it weren't for the bimonthly boon
of your consenting arms while your
husband's away on fieldwork, Fran,
I'd have that much less to croon about!
What a lot of long, cold nights that'd be
to take into the semester looming ... .

Long anticipated, predicted daily,
snowflakes begin at last to tumble,
like scraps of torn poems too paltry
ever to discombobulate a reader. Emily
sure had a point when she did her bunk.
If she reincarnates, she'll probably
choose a body far from here
and write like Charles Bukowski.

As for now
that sculpture's rattling
in harsh, post-canonical gusts
of snow
        but is too thin
to accommodate
any flake's urge
to settle.

        Not even one.

Brand

> *Tell us sir, why are you so*
> *full of shit? Now come on, Man, don't be afraid,*
> *speak right up into the microphone.*
> – Amiri Baraka ('Blue Whitie')

Can you gig it? A posture of street smarts
on the back of renounced elocution lessons,
those polite words you will no longer say
still sludging in the backyard of your mind
like church sundaes. It's just another way
to find your true home the homily, that
politically correct swagger that leads you
to more swag, brother: the incessant rap-tap
of a tap dance of clichés you always have
on tap. Harvard-hallowed, then Yaled hail!ed,
made cornier by Cornell, big toe licked slick
by every liberal who for sure will ignore
your salad days of privilege, all you now
swear not by. Isn't it fine to be downborne,
become the sister/brother/other you invoke,
after all the years of being something else?
Your ancestors were branded in their pain,
now you have conjured them into a brand
and garbled them up with your evil I ...
to parrot a poet who ponders on truth:
come, step right up to the microphone!

Laureates, at sea

The fact is some can swim

where your metaphors cannot. Your land's been uttered

so often that we despaired

of you ever planting seed in soil other than what's barren.

Now all at sea, you look

to its vastness for new spaces to journey in your heart –

but, wave-frightened,

there's mere dust rising when you want to speak of water.

What have you become?

Your fishing skiff lies rudderless, peeling paint, swarmed

by a felony of gulls

while a wind hones you, tidelorn, with so many dulled knives,

tidbits of broken songs

you half-remember; time's discarded lyrics from all the things you keep trying to love.

If you seek to voyage out further you'll fade away, diminish

into distance; poems

dragging the scarred wake of your life across endless waves

that soon will gentle it.

The reader's hypocrite

The pallor of pages wandered over
by the inked flies' feet forming the letters
of the language that you speak,
we both speak ...
                in other words,
your latest novel ...
                    and to see nothing
more than your sentences, sonorous bishops
in their flip procession across this page
where I tiptoe onwards in suspense
of what you might say
next,
     then next,
         then next,
              until my eye
              at last comes
to rest on your story's ending.

Despite my being one of those who still walks
behind the cortège of your good name, paying
homage to its limping spoors of narrative
and the scats left by the imaginary beings
you have created
          by now I find myself
sometimes trying to shake them
off my shoes –
         to confess:
         I've had enough!

Just one of many readers, I cannot help but
wonder what you've misplaced in each account,
what veneer of craft has come to hide the kernel
of this world's implacable nut, and why so many
of your words end up a fit for your own profile .…

Should I call this art?

                        For on this word-wrecked night
I suspect your hand can no longer spell out
how any of us, more needy, live
                                 but gropes around
until all ten digits lie on your keyboard comatose,
stunned by its profusion of letters,
despite your eloquence.

                        There are readers
who believe in you. But at times even you
must worry there may be those you sense,
now closing in behind you to lean over
your shoulder – still saying nothing –
who wish for tales of the lives they live
more truthful than any you can give.

Monk, dancing

for John Trimbur

It's snowing outside and the avenues
    are grey with a beauty that's been trodden on:
while inside
        the Mary Quant haircuts and short back'nsides
incline their profiles
            towards each other or the camera
    sporting glasses black and illegible
as a voided cosmos
        but then

            the drummer hits the snare
on its rim once with the backend of his stick and
    – we're off!
The mumble of drunks who won't shut up endures, scrabbling
like trapped mice but the bass
            strides where no one's looking
jiggling their tables   their manhattans and old-fashioneds
                  slop
until the drums cackle them into silence
    like a vellum hen

– though why's Monk only blocking chords?
though his grey suit's shining his brown beanie bobbing – ah

Charlie steps up to Rouse the audience
tilts his horn
              that clears its throat until
              the sound waxes gibbous and drifts down
                      into this dive's dim lighting strikes gold
      off the glitterball to spasm
into a flurry of winking stars, briefly dazzling
                      the blank
                      hip nullity
                      of every
                      watcher's eye

the rhythm
            not doing what they think they want but
maybe they'll learn

because Monk is dancing in his head
feet tap-topping-the-tap-to-toe-tap (stop that!)

white keys twinkling among the black
        between hands that may seem slabs of meat
yet the heavy ringed fingers angled against the beat
are precise on the white bones of the world:
uncovering chords, scattering notes
that swoop and dance
                    and now

Monk too
        is off his chair
                and dancing ...

Poetry

1. Poems of need

There are poems of need
that cannot be heard, and
seldom found on paper:

they may be small:
are sodden
          kittens
abandoned in rain
and left for dead,
mewling, scratched
by a wilderness
of hedge
          until
their fur clots
into small flowers
of blood
          – but you'll find
they still have claws –

or larger:
are blistered tongues
                    hanging
                out in drought, in deserts
not of their own making, that search
            among the dunes
of so many easy meanings
for any untracked path
where they can abandon
their trickery of words
and find a simpler answer,
reviving as cold water.

Poems of need put
their makers at risk:
are no help for those
who wish to move
with surer steps
                but limp
through uncanny lands
where no rising sun
will admit to its horizon
of origin

– and squint, squint
again, fearfully but
stubborn
            at the brightness
which will only
make them blind.

Poems of need
see hear smell
try to touch
try to touch

but can't feign
the life they grope
towards, somewhere
in front of them,
until its truth
appears.
        Poems of
        need are

        a tear
in back of the throat,
– a loud ripping –
at the very moment
they learn, within
themselves, there
can be no more
tears.

        Every poem of need struggles
           for its own breath …
face exhausted,
           smashed
into sleep
        in a graveyard
of silences:

although its mouth stays open.

2. Weed

The splendour of the poem
must hide its acrostics
in the puzzle of the world.
The mind alone cannot
create it, nor yet the body

... but let's leave out the page,
and its two dimensions ...

for its source is in the soil,
and a taste of earth can
give it life. This is a thought
for some as comforting
as metaphor – so, none
at all. For that's not what
I mean:

      I mean the poem
must rise up from the place
where it has lain dormant
in you, as pain and darkness
unknown and disregarded:
and will germinate from
only there
         where, in a trice,
it will weed up to choke off
those forms, those flowers
of words which, till now,
have titivated their beauty
uselessly around it.

I mean
your poem should stand up
ragged and unrepentant
so no storm nor drought
can wilt it. Look! Your
secret toil through despair
has raised up its own
new standard. At last,
your poem that is weed
is strong. Now: here's

the presence of your poem.

3. Beasts

I feel them come to me
and I do not know, again,

the form they'll take.
A moth's wraith in flight

towards light, frantic wings
knuckling on the door

of my dreams, or the snake
that slips underneath …

or a rumour of stone,
or water flowing, or fog

across a landscape that
never will be cultivated …

I lack the skill to know.
For these, my beasts,

are not subdued on waking:
they come unsummoned,

requited gifts from a heaven
fit for mutes, solitaries

who cannot hope to sing,
even as you think

they've settled and found rest
in me. Snare me

instead into the gnarled
thickets of their

meanings, hiding what
I should have learned

to discover with my lips
myself. Each slithering

shape each stinking breath
may bring dread or ardour,

as from some cat-like god
at play, batting at my skein

of words. Which may bear
some passing truth, or not –

but never comfort; never
anything I'd claim as mine.

4. *Word perfect*

Truth – that canted plank,
wobbling and warped
and full of termites,
                       flung
down for a few brief seconds
across this wallow of verse

* * *

The poet scratches his head:
thinking too often

of the bell-bodied woman
gone barefoot to the well

– the bucket she clutches
soon to become heavy –

the surprised words
have shivered, then

shimmied in rapture
right off his page

* * *

Finished for the night,
the cricket (a genius!)

packs away its sistrum,
burps one final time
                            leaves
for its home in the floorboards

no one will ever find

Clunkerfoot

In a tiled room that gleams with antiseptic
and a coat so green I can barely make out
his face
      hanging above me in anticipation

nor the two probing gloved squids he'll use
for hands
      his disembodied voice
issuing forth from a glare
of lights
      one crowned
tooth winking
familiarly at me
as he grins

      the surgeon
says:

we're giving you new hips!

This surely can't be true:

what I need to find
is some new way
of walking.

Night ward

A dark forest of sleeping
beds rustling with breath

and in each one
the squirrel of pain

has found a place
to hide its nut.

What ocean

Tides that murmur of returning,
pale light glazing on their hands,
they watch,

        this sprinkling of old men
now strolling along the pier
each one constantly in dispute
with his own body

        pause at the end
to squint mistrustfully out over
the swells and agitation
of whitecaps

and cannot help
but wonder
what looms
for them

past any horizon
they can yet see.

Mirror lost

Sit down
Let me tell you the story of smoke
- Adonis

The face is a wealthy tourist,
presumes to be given right of way:
in the stunned calm of ponds it skitters,
in any mirror where you sashay

though you know it can't stay like this
– its skin heralds your aging world –
touting the cheekbones you inhabit
though not the soul – apologetic, curled,

hidden behind the nasal cavities,
your brainpan of transient mush,
listening for tremors from the abyss,
finding those tremors it can't hush;

always imagining something better,
always wanting that little bit more,
until your bone raft finds its rock
at last, and grinds, stopped ashore

in a place you'd never reckoned,
where it's too late to be amazed
by what you've missed or disregarded:
now you're here, where a last sun flays

the features you professed. For it comes –
the scalpel's flickering above your skin,
the sudden blood clot, the carcinoma,
your heart forgetting why it stays beating.

The face spends its wealth like a tourist,
tries to savour every world it's dreamed;
but it all stops here, on this knife's edge,
where nothing is the way it seemed.

With no moment's thought

The sun retreats   from my afternoon
behind
     a conspiracy
            of clouds

another   front
     rolls in
the wind chops   at the shore
with its cleaver

white wavelets race each other
          to be stranded
they're tiny echoes of the sails

still out there
in the distance

trying to tumble
       (pitch,
      then
toss)
   their way   back
         to safety.

Stepping out

Leaving comfort

Sleeper despite the first storm:
bundles of woven reeds for a ceiling,
and a fire mutters asthmatically
inside the room making each wall glisten.
There's no conversations left that require trust,
no one brutalised outside demanding *padkos*:
the muted, threadbare sandals of the dead
no longer pass my window,
and no memory beckons.

I'm immured:
                outside my bedspread
nothing moves – until a sudden cat across
the room, a purposeful
                      flitting ginger –

and I have forgotten how to listen for
the crepitation of aging bones, or
recognise the femur of time unlatching
from the knees of friends, to render
their last journeys crippled.

Maybe soon I'll find the courage to step out
into this night, of others:
                      even the dark
has enormous rooms of succour, where
there'll be hands as yet unmet,
warm enough for me.

Against dead reckoning

Stepping out at last
broken bangles of morning light
clatter down the mountain

I keep going up

                but cannot
duck away from an outburst
of directions, intractably plural:

there is no path to be trusted here
to assuage the journey: from footstep
to footfall,
           what is there to make
believe that I, that anyone, still
has a home?

One day we will fall, together
or apart, you as well as me –

until then, no one has a lien on pain.
So lean on your pain,
                make it a friend:

take care, take all to heart,
grant every thing its sound and colour
as it moves along its own way of being.
Quieten your heart, but keep
going, forward.

              What walking is:
to recover balance.

            Each step
is its own place.

Oasis

Past Timbuktu, through the centuries,
trying to remember its wisdom
                  despite the sand
             blustered from the desert
by the sirocco
          and the savannahs drying
I dream (do you?) of an oasis, and take
comfort only because there is a place
where it still rains in my heart.

Out here, on the perimeter of thought,
at last to look up without the veil
of humankind's poisonous breath
gauzing the planet,
                where stars blaze
as the night hobbles along
                  and I leave
my footprints in a crooked line that search
for that painful new knowledge
I need to gain if I am to learn
to find my way in the dark.

As you pass by

Shoulders
shifting
to the side

        we are
that careful
not to brush
against each
other

        but I wonder:

when will
        my parched
and bitter country

be transformed by
the sweet waters
of your eyes?

What is (ode)

1

I seldom walk at the edge of the sea these days,
        venture on it even less
nor revisit the moody inexorable chafe of the waves
        – what has happened to me?
The cockleshell of my skin bobbing around me,
        uneasy saltsmell lingering
in my nose, I'm all at sea because I'm not at sea:
        no hand braces mine
though I no longer need myself apart, singular in
        the orbits I once
prided myself on choosing. But I am still erratic,
        an atom that longs
for the endless pitch and toss of tumultuous surf,
        and unlikely voyages.

Sometimes, in this small town, I find the best table
        to put my body
down beside others, be served coffee and croissants,
        and believe my life
still matters enough to be eaten, slowly sweetened,
        even as trucks whizz by
to döppler inside my ears, promising escape to all
        that's undefined and distant,
punctuated by the stirring of relentless teaspoons
        chattering in their cups …

but it's distraction, just distraction with no purpose.
>   Belief is an easy menu
to select: the faux sympathy that prompts a tip thrust
>   at a waiter's rote concern;
as are the prepacked meals full of ideologies I once
>   thought I had chosen
– was once beguiled by – that promised every kind
>   of outcome but not
the disappointments they enacted: wordploys hiding
>   the constant command
to *listen, but don't speak!* until my deference started
>   choking me repeatedly.

Even now I'm chary to cause offence with any truth,
>   but stay undetected
even as revulsion still moles into my earth and blights
>   any harvest. My people
have fallen from my pockets like small change, lost
>   in tangles of falsehood
that have taken root: undergrowths of suspicion that
>   serve to trip us up.

The clever words I'd penned for years lift their upstrokes
>   like alarmed warthog tails,
and disappear over time's horizon. So these days I must
>   trick things out myself
with only my trove of past failures: those heaps of rotted
>   artefacts piled up in
the attic of memory, artfully suspended over my mistakes
>   and the love hotels
in which I've slept. Home? - Ramshackled, tended only by
>   a few last pieties,

evacuated a long time since and slowly unhinging, nail
        on nail. Outside, gardens
of paper flowers stand-in for lost beauty, fake perfumes
        which charm no life.

2

To survive these days my head turns around on my neck
        like an owl, sensing
danger. Such a fickle compass! In droughts and in winds
        of hopeless poverty
the lives around me lived next to city malls seem endless,
        flies stuck in amber.
Chosen words no longer stride out of now-barricaded doors
        to face oppression
but birth our ancestors as our children, fitfully redeemed by
        swarms of mythologies
while a 'revolution' ignorant of all community primps
        by on tottering
Gucci steps, eructates from every shop and fashion
        website, pretends
to be striding towards some future advent of equality.
        But Liberation brought
in its wake new variants of control, salespeople with
        false guarantees, blue
light cavalcades ablare with fraudsters evoking heroes
        who, were they alive,
would only have despised them. A diversity of hashtags
        rise up into the cloud,
jostling and bickering, people intent on saving the little
        that they still have:
townhouses and highrises scab across the land above

a skin of shacks,
the city's face pocked with cancroid growths where we
    eke out our lives.
What's left to us, neglectful, demanding, unquestioning?
    How do we unwind
this clocklike world of disparity and disillusion, find
    what was promised?

3

For this is what they told us: *"Your hopes will flurry dust*
    even if there's rain,
because the pools that lay siege to your shelters flood there
    only because the rivers
that bring down brown letters from the bowels of the rich
    for you to read
clog up with rubbish. Pyramids of cans surround each home
    but emptied of their
Gods – hear them rattle their dead bones in every breeze –
    though they may
glint from time to time with light borrowed from all our
    unfulfilled promises.
And you? If you hear, but can no longer speak of need,
    it's because your tongues
have been cut out by the sharp edge of our soft sympathy."

        … So the woke humans
we claim to be blink and blear in each morning's sun,
    swap fricatives
and glottals that click into gossip about each other.
    It is unbearable
to hear again the old dead stories we're used to telling

    reignited as if new,
as we reconstruct wounds from others that make us
    sputter still with
vindictiveness, laced through with spite, then watch
    the ancient venom
traces its way in bodies ripe for rot through our veins
    to reach at last
our hearts; as if to wear wounds in words were truly
    to be wounded.

My country: a sickened bird in moult, its difficult birthing
    stalled in nests
of privilege, where the rich fledge their lies in concord
    with their former
enemies while preaching on interminably of righteousness.
    So, we prevaricate,
await dissolution. Or whatever a further day's survival
    demands of us.
Birds build nests in a maze of building sites, the sea curls back
    to mire the shore
with pearls of plastic for the swine who first fashioned them:
    bureaucratic edicts
fabricate plans for structures which multiply into an infinite
    wilderness where
half-built homes thrum, hollowed out of what was put there
    until pillaged.
Who can steal it back, find ways to rebuild so many desolate
    places? Like you
I want comfort, but not at the expense of a window's view
    outwards onto mere
assurances, as we continue peering at shards of light framed
    between barbed wire,

all the while that suited tender-minded thieves feed upon
    the corpses of
a rotten State and its benighted Party until we squeal
    "we are betrayed!",
as if we could not have seen this future coming.

4

    It's a fact that
history seems to take us all hostage in the end. Should I
    now rehearse again
the terms of my (your?) surrender? We keep dying but
    our verbs repeat,
child after child – the geegaws of the wealthy always
    that distracted us
now begin to destroy the planet. Who can enjoy seasons
    returning when
they come with drying fields, our skylines hazed with filth,
    all these poisoned
harvestings? Sometimes we peer out, and find ourselves
    in a present
that may as well just be the past, because all our futures
    have been cut off.

Still I feel my anger rise up as language to haemorrhage
    my smile, snipe from
my lips, in hope what comes out may seem close to true.
    But does this work?
I don't long for a day of just deserts I don't long for
    executions. But what
recurs are words abused by us, their owners, who guard
    themselves with homilies

that cause tongues to bloat and stiffen, one by one,
    in mortuaries of fear.
If we wait too long all will be lost, for there is little
    free ground left.
And tonight it's no subtle wind that blows its hot cinders
    onto my arms
from a nearby fire that silhouettes a throng of running
    figures in despair
who gyrate around its centre, trying to save something,
    anything at all,
of the meagre objects which they still cling onto despite
    their dispossession.

5

There was a time when justice - that weighty word! -
    was freed up
to toy with all our mouths. There was a chance, once,
    for something.
The blood could still be seen, yes, but had congealed
    and it was like
the earth was for a moment silent, as in anticipation.
    But I think, now,
that justice is a bird that will not fly till it is fledged
    by all our mouths.
And how, without it, will we learn to love? To know
    what love might be,
beyond an aching in our flesh; more than ten fingers
    held out hoping
for another's solace – held, but always to be loosened:
    beyond the habitual
bedposts' dance; beyond the loss of love through pain
    or dread or worry.

There are questions that never cease to ask themselves,
  that the days
of solidarity and sacrifice once felt free to demand
  of everyone.
As for me, I live in error yet, not knowing what I owe.
  I still toil
to scatter my country's ashes further into the broad seas
  of humanity, but
can no longer make out if its borders are where faith
  says they should
be. Now it's later; and a cutting edge of moon rises to
  illumine the lonely
clamour of a distant peacock afoot despite the dark,
  vaunting its avowal
of belonging. And there are those who also start to lift
  their faces, wonder
when it will be time to look for light that reveals a new
  horizon. For this life
I've lived has shown me to live must mean to think,
  what is owed?
then risk oneself for others: for all those still at risk.

Gaze

Blinded each day
by sun

       no one sees
that the blue eggshell
of the sky

       is salted
with stars.

Kelwyn Sole was born in Johannesburg in 1951 and was educated there and in London. He worked as a school teacher in Botswana, managed an education programme in Namibia and designed and oversaw the writing of a set of *History of Africa* books for an anti-apartheid N.G.O. in Johannesburg. Thereafter, he spent 30 years at the University of Cape Town, lecturing on African and South African literature, Seventeen-Century English poetry and Western and global modernisms in the Department of English Language and Literature; eventually becoming the De Beers Professor.

Sole has written many critical articles on South African and postcolonial literature in local and international books and journals, and his poetry has been widely anthologised. Critical articles of his have won the Thomas Pringle and AA Mutual Life/Vita Awards. His first collection of poetry *The Blood of Our Silence* won the Olive Schreiner Prize and his seventh, *Walking, Falling* the South African Literary Award (SALA) for Poetry. His most recent collection *Skin Rafts* was shortlisted for the National Institute for the Humanities & Social Sciences (NHSS) Award. Over the years, individual poems have won the DALRO, Thomas Pringle and Sydney Clouts Awards.

What Is Owed? is his ninth collection of poetry.

Kelwyn Sole Previous Collections

The Blood of Our Silence (Johannesburg: Ravan Press, 1988)
Projections in the Past Tense (Johannesburg: Ravan Press, 1992)
Love That is Night (Durban: Gecko Poetry, 1998)
Mirror and Water Gazing (Scottsville: Gecko/University of Natal Press, 2001)
Land Dreaming: prose poems
(Scottsville: University of Kwazulu-Natal Press, 2006)
Absent Tongues (Cape Town: Hands-On Books, 2012)
Walking, Falling (Makhanda: Deep South, 2017)
Skin Rafts (Cape Town: Hands-On Books, 2022)

Botsotso Poetry since 2016

Songs of Tenderness and Dread – Abu Bakr Solomons
Loud and Yellow Laughter – Sindiswa Bususku-Mathese
The Colours of Our Flag – Allan Kolski Horwitz
The Alkalinity of Bottled Water – Makhosazana Xaba
On Days Such as This – Gail Dendy
Inhibiting Love – Abu Bakr Solomons
A History of Disappearance – Sarah Lubala
Hungry on Arrival – Kabelo Mofokeng
U Grand, Malume? – Sizakele Nkosi
Zabalaza Republic – Sihle Ntuli
Studies in Khoisan Verbs and other poems – Basil du Toit
Everybody is a Bridge – Anton Krueger
Igoli Egoli – Salimah Valiani
Down the Baakens Underworld – Brian Walter
A place to night in – Frank Meintjies
Flight of the Bird Spirit – Richard Cullinan
Maxwell the Gorilla and the Archbishop of Soshanguve – Angifi Proctor Dlaldla
Notes from the Dream Kingdom – KG Goddard
Rubble – Abu Bakr Solomons
Inside an Eyelid – Zeenat Saban-Jacobs

www.ingramcontent.com/pod-product-compliance
Lightning Source LLC
Chambersburg PA
CBHW050915160426
43194CB00011B/2410